known

God Knows When You Feel Anxious

Psalms 1-30

A Bible Study by

Lisa Toney

WH♥LEHEARTED
DEVOTION *Series*

Known
God Knows When You Feel Anxious

ISBN 979-8-8598-1149-6

Manufactured in the United States of America

TABLE OF

CONTENTS

About The Author

Lisa Toney is a popular speaker and author who points people to Jesus. She is a professor of Spiritual Formation at Hope International University in Fullerton, CA. Lisa holds a Communications degree from Taylor University and a Master of Divinity degree from Fuller Theological Seminary. Lisa enjoys teaching and encouraging people at nationwide and international conferences and events. She hosts the Faith Habits for Success YouTube show and podcast. Lisa and her husband often lead trips to the Bible lands, including Israel, Greece, Italy, and Turkey, with InspireTravelGroup.org. Lisa served on the preaching and pastoral teams of a large Southern California church for 20 years. Lisa and her husband, Carl, are raising four amazing kids: five chickens, one puppy, and one gecko. She loves sailing, swimming, coffee, dark chocolate, and is a big fan of The Chosen series.

Be friends with Lisa!

 @LisaToneyLife

 Lisa Toney

 Lisa Toney

 Faith Habits For Success

 LisaToney.com

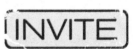

Lisa loves meeting new people and bringing a Jesus-centered, Bible-based, high-energy message of encouragement. Invite her to speak at your next event!

lisatoney.com/invite

Live Bold. **Love** Big. **Lead** Wise.
Lisa Toney - Faith Habits

About The Psalms

Hebrew: תְּהִלִּים, *Tehillim*, "praises"

150 Psalms

Composed over **1000** years

73 Psalms are authored by King David

More than **7** different authors

Jesus quotes the Psalms more than any other book.

1010-930 BC   *Authors*

Most Psalms were written during the time of David and his son Solomon.

- David (73 Psalms)
- Asaph (and family) (12 Psalms): 50; 73—83
- The sons of Korah (11 Psalms): 42; 44—49; 84—85; 87—88
- Heman (1 Psalm, with the sons of Korah): 88
- Solomon (2 Psalms): 72 and 127
- Moses (1 Psalm): 90
- Ethan the Ezrahite (1 Psalm): 89
- Anonymous (the 48 remaining Psalms)

Some of the different types of Psalms are thanksgiving, wisdom, lament, royal, trust, praise, prophecy, pilgrimage, infliction, and temple hymns.

The Psalms were collected as a prayer book for God's people as they waited for the arrival of the Messiah and the fulfillment of God's promises.

The Lord Is My Shepherd

WH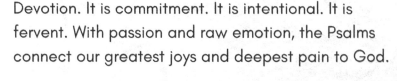LEHEARTED DEVOTION *Series*

Devotion. It is commitment. It is intentional. It is fervent. With passion and raw emotion, the Psalms connect our greatest joys and deepest pain to God.

The Wholehearted Devotion Series is a set of Bible Study studies that take you through the book of Psalms. Each study is six weeks. You will go through 30 Psalms in each of the five studies.

KNOWN – Psalms 1-30
SEEN – Psalms 31-60
HEARD – Psalms 61-90
LOVED – Psalms 91-120
UNDERSTOOD – Psalms 121-150

As we journey through the Psalms, we will find the glistening gold in the names of God, the emotional depths of our souls, and the rich contrast between God's ways and those of this world.

With wholehearted devotion, we are seeking to KNOW God. We will get close. We will connect our lives with the God of the Psalms with wholehearted devotion. We are about to strike gold, my friend.

whole·heart·ed

marked by complete earnest **commitment**:

free from all reserve or hesitation

Theme Verse

May I wh♥leheartedly follow your decrees.
Psalm 119:80

known

GOD KNOWS WHEN YOU ARE ANXIOUS

Welcome to **KNOWN**: God Knows When You Are Anxious! This is the first in the Wholehearted Devotion Series and covers Psalms 1-30.

It's pretty amazing to think that God knows us, right? Each of us! God knows and loves deeply. In a world of 8 billion people, that blows my mind.

In this study, we will dive into the Psalms and marvel at the beauty and poetry of this book. We will also see the raw emotion of the Psalmists as they write. Through their words, we will connect our lives and emotions to God. We will see how being KNOWN by God is powerful. It can quiet our anxiety and restore our confidence even amid the unknown. I can't wait to see what God does!

Theme Verse

You make **KNOWN** to
me the path of life;
You will fill me with joy
in your presence,
with eternal pleasures
at your right hand.

Psalm 16:11

What Do I Need To Know?

Bible Recommendation: You can use any Bible you love, but Pastor Lisa recommends the *NIV & The Message Side-By-Side Bible* for this study. This puts two translations right next to one another and is helpful for study. *The Message* translation is written in the modern-day vernacular and captures the beauty of the poetry of the Psalms. Pastor Lisa will be referring to this translation often in this study.

You'll want your Bible, this workbook, and a pen to take weekly notes during the teaching time. Pastor Lisa brings a message centered around one of the Psalms each week. There is a page at the beginning of each weekly section to take notes. After the teaching time, there are questions for discussion with your small group. Honestly, this is the best part! It is where you share what is happening in your life, how God is working, what you are learning in this study, build friendships with other women, and pray for one another.

Video Access: With the purchase of this book you also have access to the streaming video teaching with Lisa Toney. To access your video content, go to LisaToney.com/knownaccess or scan the QR code at the bottom of each teaching notes page.

Each week, you have one **Focus Verse** and five **Daily Strategies**. These allow you to engage with the Psalms and connect your life with God. Each day, you will read one Psalm. Then, there is a selected verse from that Psalm for you to spend a few minutes with. On the next page, I will teach you my Engagement Strategy, a simple but powerful way to talk to God and let Him talk to you through Scripture. It's a really good way to feel **KNOWN** by God.

How do I use a weekly
Focus Verse?

Each week, I will give you one focus verse. This is a verse that I want you to keep top of mind. You may try to memorize it. You may put it on your phone as your screensaver. You can say it out loud every day. You can talk about it with your friends and family.

Your focus verse is meant to keep your heart and mind focused on that TRUTH all week.

Don't worry; there is no test on this. It is for your encouragement and spiritual growth. Exercise those spiritual muscles and hide God's Word in your heart. It is a powerful protection, defense against the enemy, decision-making aid, relationship strengthener, and all-around God-honoring strategy to learn these focus verses!

Learn them. Live them.

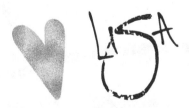

12

YOUR *Daily Strategy*

Each day, you will have the opportunity to read one Psalm. This will be an amazing chance to encourage daily Bible reading as your daily Faith Habit.

Practicing **The Prayer of Connection** with one verse in the Psalm you read is part of your daily strategy to connect with God.

THE PRAYER OF CONNECTION

I created **The Prayer of Connection** to help me learn how to connect my daily life with God through Scripture. It doesn't take long, but it sure is powerful. It will help you build an intimate relationship with Jesus where you feel seen, heard, and known. I can't wait for you to try it.

It has six parts or phases that you do with just one or two verses that will be highlighted for you on your Daily Strategy page. This will help you connect your life with God.

THE PRAYER OF C⊗NNECTION

PRINT

Write out your daily strategy focus verse so that you start to help your brain engage with it in a different way than reading it silently on the page.

PRONOUNCE

Say your daily strategy focus verse out loud so that you hear the words and continue to help your brain engage the verse by concentrating on it.

PAUSE

This time, read the verse out loud again, but pause on each phrase or word. This helps you to slow your roll and begin to hone in on the meanings of the words and ideas.

PINPOINT

Circle, underline, or highlight any words or phrases that jump out to you as you look at this verse. There is no right or wrong here, just what you notice.

PERSONALIZE

Write out the phrases of the verse, and after each phrase write out your life events that connect with that phrase. You can write out any ideas that come to mind. You want to be very specific.

POUR

Now turn the life events you just listed into a prayer. Pour your heart out to the Lord using the Scripture and the things that you personalized. This is your opportunity for deep connection.

The following pages provide a sample of *The Prayer Of Connection*.

1. **Print** the verse by writing it out

Trouble and distress have come upon me, but your commands give me delight.

Psalm 119:143

Sample

2.Pronounce the verse by saying it out loud

Trouble and distress have come upon me, but your commands give me delight.

Psalm 119:143

16

3. <u>Pause on each phrase</u>

Trouble — and distress —
have come upon — ME —
but — your commands —
give
me
delight.

Psalm 119:143

4. <u>Pinpoint</u> each word that stands out to you

(Trouble) and distress have come upon me, but (your) commands give me (delight).

Psalm 119:143

5. Personalize by listing your life events in each phrase

Trouble and distress have come upon me

I am mourning the loss of my Dad to cancer – I hate cancer
I am not sure what to do about one of my child's behavior
I am so upset that someone was talking about me behind my back.
How long will our van hold out before we need a new one?

but

I really like this word.
It means there is change – a transition – things won't stay the same

your commands

Your words to me. Your ideas. Your thoughts.
Your plans for my life. Your instructions to me.

give me

I love when people give me things! I love to give others things. YOU GOD are going to give ME something? Amazing. I'm in!

Lisa Huber Toney

delight.

I love this word. Delight. Joy. Joy comes in the morning. I want to live with delight. I want the joy. The joy of the Lord WILL be my strength. I want to be a person that delights in the Lord.

6. Pour out your heart by praying your life events with each phrase

Trouble and distress have come upon me

Lord, I miss my Dad. I miss talking with him. I miss having him around. It all went so fast. Please help me and my sisters and mom with our grief. May you heal our hurting hearts. Jesus, please give me wisdom about what to do with this child that is acting out. I don't know how to best encourage, love, correct, and direct – but I know you do. Show me what to do.

Help me to forgive those talking about me. Show me what I can do to represent you well. Please help us trust you to provide all that we need – even a new van in your timing.

but

I love this word, Lord. It means that you are working. You are moving. Things are not going to remain the same. Help me to trust you Lord. Bring your power and change and hope and healing into my life.

your commands

Help me to trust your commands. Fill my mind and heart with your truth. Let your wisdom guide my life. Instruct me. Teach me. Shape me. Mold me. May you be the light for my steps.

give me

Thank you that are a giver. You give good gifts. You are a good and gracious God. Help me to live with my hands open to what you want to give rather than closed fisted over what I have.

delight.

Lisa Huber Toney. Little ole' me. You see me. You know me. You care. Oh yeah! Amen and Hallelujah! I'm leaning into this. Delight! You have delight for ME! I love me some delight. Joy. Joy in the morning. The joy of the Lord is my strength. Thank you that You restore my soul. Thank you for bringing delight when I least expect it but most need it. You are a God who delights in delighting your children. Thank you, sweet Jesus! Amen!

Answers

Psalms 1–5

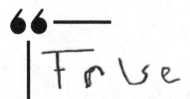

True

The right way to answer
'true and false 'questions

Learn With Lisa
WK 1 Teaching Notes

Answers

The Answer
By Jeremy Camp

Talk & Share

Discussion Questions:

1. Introduce yourself and share about your family.

2. Why did you decide to participate in this Bible study?

3. Who do you think knows you best?

4. How does the idea of being known by God bring you comfort?

5. What answers are you seeking from God right now?

Focus Verse

But You, Lord,
are a shield around me, my glory,
the One who lifts my head high.
Psalm 3:3

Create

What answers are you seeking?
- Write a poem or song asking your questions and finding answers in Jesus.
- Make a list of questions you've had answered from God.
- Draw or paint an expression of Jesus being the beginning and the end.
- Build something that is the answer to a need.

Care

Answer someone.
- Answer a question with absolute patience.
- Be the answer before someone asks.
- Answer someone's doubts with your confidence that the Lord is working.

Focus Verse

1. Find a quiet place to sit with your Bible and journal.

2. Close your eyes, take a deep breath, invite Jesus to center you in His truth and hold you in His love with this exercise:

- ○ Put your hands together, fingers pointing away from you, and say:
  Center me in Your truth.
- ○ Fold your hands together, squeeze, and say:
  Hold me in Your love.
- ○ Take another deep breath, open your eyes.

Read your focus verse for the week.
Say your focus verse for the week.
Write your focus verse for the week.

Daily Strategy

Read Psalms Chapter 1

Work with this verse: Psalm 1:1-2

1. **Print:** Write out the verse(s)
2. **Pronounce**: Read the verse(s) out loud
3. **Pause**: Reread the verse(s) and pause on each word or phrase
4. **Pinpoint:** Circle or underline the words that jump out at you
5. **Personalize:** Place your life events into each phrase
6. **Pour:** Write each section you personalized into a prayer

Use this space below or your own prayer journal.

Focus Verse

1. Find a quiet place to sit with your Bible and journal.

2. Close your eyes, take a deep breath, invite Jesus to center you in His truth and hold you in His love with this exercise:

- Put your hands together, fingers pointing away from you, and say:
  Center me in Your truth.
- Fold your hands together, squeeze, and say:
  Hold me in Your love.
- Take another deep breath, open your eyes.

Read your focus verse for the week.
Say your focus verse for the week.
Write your focus verse for the week.

Daily Strategy

Read Psalms Chapter 2

Work with this verse: Psalm 2:8

1. **Print:** Write out the verse(s)
2. **Pronounce**: Read the verse(s) out loud
3. **Pause**: Reread the verse(s) and pause on each word or phrase
4. **Pinpoint:** Circle or underline the words that jump out at you
5. **Personalize:** Place your life events into each phrase
6. **Pour:** Write each section you personalized into a prayer

Use this space below or your own prayer journal.

Focus Verse

1. Find a quiet place to sit with your Bible and journal.

2. Close your eyes, take a deep breath, invite Jesus to center you in His truth and hold you in His love with this exercise:

- Put your hands together, fingers pointing away from you, and say:
  Center me in Your truth.
- Fold your hands together, squeeze, and say:
  Hold me in Your love.
- Take another deep breath, open your eyes.

Read your focus verse for the week.
Say your focus verse for the week.
Write your focus verse for the week.

Daily Strategy

Read Psalms Chapter 3

Work with this verse: Psalm 3:3

1. **Print:** Write out the verse(s)
2. **Pronounce**: Read the verse(s) out loud
3. **Pause**: Reread the verse(s) and pause on each word or phrase
4. **Pinpoint:** Circle or underline the words that jump out at you
5. **Personalize:** Place your life events into each phrase
6. **Pour:** Write each section you personalized into a prayer

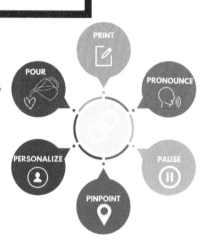

Use this space below or your own prayer journal.

Focus Verse

1. Find a quiet place to sit with your Bible and journal.

2.Close your eyes, take a deep breath, invite Jesus to center you in His truth and hold you in His love with this exercise:

- o Put your hands together, fingers pointing away from you, and say:
  Center me in Your truth.
- o Fold your hands together, squeeze, and say:
  Hold me in Your love.
- o Take another deep breath, open your eyes.

Read your focus verse for the week.

Say your focus verse for the week.

Write your focus verse for the week.

WH♥LEHEARTED DEVOTION *Series*

GOD KNOWS WHEN YOU ARE ANXIOUS

Daily Strategy

Read Psalms Chapter 4

Work with this verse: Psalm 4:1

1. **Print:** Write out the verse(s)
2. **Pronounce**: Read the verse(s) out loud
3. **Pause**: Reread the verse(s) and pause on each word or phrase
4. **Pinpoint:** Circle or underline the words that jump out at you
5. **Personalize:** Place your life events into each phrase
6. **Pour:** Write each section you personalized into a prayer

Use this space below or your own prayer journal.

Focus Verse

1. Find a quiet place to sit with your Bible and journal.

2. Close your eyes, take a deep breath, invite Jesus to center you in His truth and hold you in His love with this exercise:

- Put your hands together, fingers pointing away from you, and say:
  Center me in Your truth.
- Fold your hands together, squeeze, and say:
  Hold me in Your love.
- Take another deep breath, open your eyes.

Read your focus verse for the week.
Say your focus verse for the week.
Write your focus verse for the week.

WH♥LEHEARTED DEVOTION *Series*

Daily Strategy

Read Psalms Chapter 5

Work with this verse: Psalm 5:11

1. **Print:** Write out the verse(s)
2. **Pronounce**: Read the verse(s) out loud
3. **Pause**: Reread the verse(s) and pause on each word or phrase
4. **Pinpoint:** Circle or underline the words that jump out at you
5. **Personalize:** Place your life events into each phrase
6. **Pour:** Write each section you personalized into a prayer

PRINT
PRONOUNCE
POUR
PAUSE
PERSONALIZE
PINPOINT

Use this space below or your own prayer journal.

Week 2

Thankful

Psalms 6-10

" —

THE THING I AM MOST THANKFUL FOR RIGHT NOW IS STRETCHY WAISTBANDS.

Ha Ha Ha Ha Ha

Learn With Lisa
WK 2 Teaching Notes

Thankful

**Thank You Jesus
For The Blood**
By Charity Gayle

Talk & Share

Discussion Questions:

1. What was most impactful to you as you read the Psalms last week?

2. What emotions did you connect with as you read the Psalms?

3. What are some things you are most thankful for right now?

4. Where do you need God to show up for you this week?

5. What is one word that you would use to describe God from your time in the Psalms this week?

Focus Verse

I will give thanks to you, Lord,
with all my heart; I will tell
of all Your wonderful deeds.

Psalm 9:1

Create

What are you thankful to God for?

- Write a poem or song describing your thankfulness to God.
- Make a gratitude journal and write five things you are thankful for each day.
- Draw or paint an expression of your thankful heart.
- Build something that you can give to someone as a thank-you!

Care

Thank someone

- Send a handwritten thank-you note.
- Write a text to a friend thanking them in specific ways for how they bless your life.
- Thank a service person who delivers your mail, picks up your trash, or delivers packages or groceries.

Focus Verse

1. Find a quiet place to sit with your Bible and journal.

2. Close your eyes, take a deep breath, invite Jesus to center you in His truth and hold you in His love with this exercise:

- Put your hands together, fingers pointing away from you, and say:
  Center me in Your truth.
- Fold your hands together, squeeze, and say:
  Hold me in Your love.
- Take another deep breath, open your eyes.

Read your focus verse for the week.

Say your focus verse for the week.

Write your focus verse for the week.

Daily Strategy

Read Psalms Chapter 6

Work with this verse: Psalm 6:4

1. **Print:** Write out the verse(s)
2. **Pronounce**: Read the verse(s) out loud
3. **Pause**: Reread the verse(s) and pause on each word or phrase
4. **Pinpoint:** Circle or underline the words that jump out at you
5. **Personalize:** Place your life events into each phrase
6. **Pour:** Write each section you personalized into a prayer

Use this space below or your own prayer journal.

Focus Verse

1. Find a quiet place to sit with your Bible and journal.

2. Close your eyes, take a deep breath, invite Jesus to center you in His truth and hold you in His love with this exercise:

- o   Put your hands together, fingers pointing away from you, and say:
     Center me in Your truth.
- o   Fold your hands together, squeeze, and say:
     Hold me in Your love.
- o   Take another deep breath, open your eyes.

Read your focus verse for the week.

Say your focus verse for the week.

Write your focus verse for the week.

Daily Strategy

Read Psalms Chapter 7

Work with this verse: Psalm 7:17

1. **Print:** Write out the verse(s)
2. **Pronounce**: Read the verse(s) out loud
3. **Pause**: Reread the verse(s) and pause on each word or phrase
4. **Pinpoint:** Circle or underline the words that jump out at you
5. **Personalize:** Place your life events into each phrase
6. **Pour:** Write each section you personalized into a prayer

Use this space below or your own prayer journal.

Focus Verse

1. Find a quiet place to sit with your Bible and journal.

2. Close your eyes, take a deep breath, invite Jesus to center you in His truth and hold you in His love with this exercise:

- ○ Put your hands together, fingers pointing away from you, and say:
  Center me in Your truth.

- ○ Fold your hands together, squeeze, and say:
  Hold me in Your love.

- ○ Take another deep breath, open your eyes.

Read your focus verse for the week.

Say your focus verse for the week.

Write your focus verse for the week.

Daily Strategy

Read Psalms Chapter 8

Work with this verse: Psalm 8:2

1. **Print:** Write out the verse(s)
2. **Pronounce:** Read the verse(s) out loud
3. **Pause:** Reread the verse(s) and pause on each word or phrase
4. **Pinpoint:** Circle or underline the words that jump out at you
5. **Personalize:** Place your life events into each phrase
6. **Pour:** Write each section you personalized into a prayer

Use this space below or your own prayer journal.

Focus Verse

1. Find a quiet place to sit with your Bible and journal.

2. Close your eyes, take a deep breath, invite Jesus to center you in His truth and hold you in His love with this exercise:

- ○ Put your hands together, fingers pointing away from you, and say:
  Center me in Your truth.
- ○ Fold your hands together, squeeze, and say:
  Hold me in Your love.
- ○ Take another deep breath, open your eyes.

Read your focus verse for the week.

Say your focus verse for the week.

Write your focus verse for the week.

Daily Strategy

Read Psalms Chapter 9

Work with this verse: Psalm 9:1

1. **Print:** Write out the verse(s)
2. **Pronounce**: Read the verse(s) out loud
3. **Pause**: Reread the verse(s) and pause on each word or phrase
4. **Pinpoint:** Circle or underline the words that jump out at you
5. **Personalize:** Place your life events into each phrase
6. **Pour:** Write each section you personalized into a prayer

Use this space below or your own prayer journal.

Focus Verse

1. Find a quiet place to sit with your Bible and journal.

2. Close your eyes, take a deep breath, invite Jesus to center you in His truth and hold you in His love with this exercise:

- Put your hands together, fingers pointing away from you, and say:

  Center me in Your truth.

- Fold your hands together, squeeze, and say:

  Hold me in Your love.

- Take another deep breath, open your eyes.

Read your focus verse for the week.

Say your focus verse for the week.

Write your focus verse for the week.

Daily Strategy

Read Psalms Chapter 10

Work with this verse: Psalm 10:14

1. **Print:** Write out the verse(s)
2. **Pronounce**: Read the verse(s) out loud
3. **Pause**: Reread the verse(s) and pause on each word or phrase
4. **Pinpoint:** Circle or underline the words that jump out at you
5. **Personalize:** Place your life events into each phrase
6. **Pour:** Write each section you personalized into a prayer

Use this space below or your own prayer journal.

PRINT

POUR

PRONOUNCE

PERSONALIZE

PAUSE

PINPOINT

Week 3

Move

Psalms 10–15

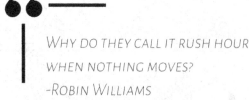

*Why do they call it rush hour
when nothing moves?*
-Robin Williams

Learn With Lisa
WK 3 Teaching Notes

God Is On The Move
By 7eventh Time Down

Talk & Share

Discussion Questions:

1. What was most impactful to you as you read the Psalms last week?

2. What emotions did you connect with as you read the Psalms?

3. Where do you see God on the move in your life?

4. How do you live differently knowing that God is working behind the scenes and moving even when you can't see it?

5. Where do you need God to show up for you this week?

Focus Verse

But I trust in Your unfailing love;
my heart rejoices in Your salvation.
Psalm 13:5

Create

How is God on the move in your life?

- Write a poem or song describing how God is on the move.
- Make a vision board and track God's movements.
- Draw or paint an expression of the movement of God.
- Build something that moves you with a thankful heart.

Care

Move someone towards God.

- Walk with someone and ask them where they see God moving in their life.
- Do you now someone moving? Help them pack or take some food over when their kitchen is packed.
- Move out some unused things and donate them to a thrift store for others to use.

Focus Verse

1. Find a quiet place to sit with your Bible and journal.

2. Close your eyes, take a deep breath, invite Jesus to center you in His truth and hold you in His love with this exercise:

- Put your hands together, fingers pointing away from you, and say:
  Center me in Your truth.
- Fold your hands together, squeeze, and say:
  Hold me in Your love.
- Take another deep breath, open your eyes.

Read your focus verse for the week.
Say your focus verse for the week.
Write your focus verse for the week.

Daily Strategy

Read Psalms Chapter 11

Work with this verse: Psalm 11:7

1. **Print:** Write out the verse(s)
2. **Pronounce**: Read the verse(s) out loud
3. **Pause**: Reread the verse(s) and pause on each word or phrase
4. **Pinpoint:** Circle or underline the words that jump out at you
5. **Personalize:** Place your life events into each phrase
6. **Pour:** Write each section you personalized into a prayer

Use this space below or your own prayer journal.

Focus Verse

1. Find a quiet place to sit with your Bible and journal.

2. Close your eyes, take a deep breath, invite Jesus to center you in His truth and hold you in His love with this exercise:

- Put your hands together, fingers pointing away from you, and say:
  Center me in Your truth.
- Fold your hands together, squeeze, and say:
  Hold me in Your love.
- Take another deep breath, open your eyes.

Read your focus verse for the week.
Say your focus verse for the week.
Write your focus verse for the week.

Daily Strategy

Read Psalms Chapter 12

Work with this verse: Psalm 12:7-8

1. **Print:** Write out the verse(s)
2. **Pronounce**: Read the verse(s) out loud
3. **Pause**: Reread the verse(s) and pause on each word or phrase
4. **Pinpoint:** Circle or underline the words that jump out at you
5. **Personalize:** Place your life events into each phrase
6. **Pour:** Write each section you personalized into a prayer

Use this space below or your own prayer journal.

Focus Verse

1. Find a quiet place to sit with your Bible and journal.

2. Close your eyes, take a deep breath, invite Jesus to center you in His truth and hold you in His love with this exercise:

- o Put your hands together, fingers pointing away from you, and say:
  Center me in Your truth.
- o Fold your hands together, squeeze, and say:
  Hold me in Your love.
- o Take another deep breath, open your eyes.

Read your focus verse for the week.

Say your focus verse for the week.

Write your focus verse for the week.

Daily Strategy

Read Psalms Chapter 13

Work with this verse: Psalm 13:5

1. **Print:** Write out the verse(s)
2. **Pronounce**: Read the verse(s) out loud
3. **Pause**: Reread the verse(s) and pause on each word or phrase
4. **Pinpoint:** Circle or underline the words that jump out at you
5. **Personalize:** Place your life events into each phrase
6. **Pour:** Write each section you personalized into a prayer

Use this space below or your own prayer journal.

Focus Verse

1. Find a quiet place to sit with your Bible and journal.

2. Close your eyes, take a deep breath, invite Jesus to center you in His truth and hold you in His love with this exercise:

- Put your hands together, fingers pointing away from you, and say:
  Center me in Your truth.
- Fold your hands together, squeeze, and say:
  Hold me in Your love.
- Take another deep breath, open your eyes.

Read your focus verse for the week.
Say your focus verse for the week.
Write your focus verse for the week.

Daily Strategy

Read Psalms Chapter 14

Work with this verse: Psalm 14:2

1. **Print:** Write out the verse(s)
2. **Pronounce**: Read the verse(s) out loud
3. **Pause**: Reread the verse(s) and pause on each word or phrase
4. **Pinpoint:** Circle or underline the words that jump out at you
5. **Personalize:** Place your life events into each phrase
6. **Pour:** Write each section you personalized into a prayer

Use this space below or your own prayer journal.

Focus Verse

1. Find a quiet place to sit with your Bible and journal.

2. Close your eyes, take a deep breath, invite Jesus to center you in His truth and hold you in His love with this exercise:

- Put your hands together, fingers pointing away from you, and say:
  Center me in Your truth.
- Fold your hands together, squeeze, and say:
  Hold me in Your love.
- Take another deep breath, open your eyes.

Read your focus verse for the week.

Say your focus verse for the week.

Write your focus verse for the week.

Daily Strategy

Read Psalms Chapter 15

Work with this verse: Psalm 15:1-2

1. **Print:** Write out the verse(s)
2. **Pronounce**: Read the verse(s) out loud
3. **Pause**: Reread the verse(s) and pause on each word or phrase
4. **Pinpoint:** Circle or underline the words that jump out at you
5. **Personalize:** Place your life events into each phrase
6. **Pour:** Write each section you personalized into a prayer

Use this space below or your own prayer journal.

Week 4

Rescue

Psalms 16-20

" —

I'M NOT A PRINCESS THAT NEEDS
TO BE RESCUED. I'M A QUEEN
AND I'VE GOT THIS HANDLED.

Ha Ha Ha
Ha Ha

WK 4
Rescue

Rescue Story
By Zach Williams

Talk & Share

Discussion Questions:

1. What Psalm spoke to your heart the most this week?

2. How is the poetry of the Psalms connecting with you?

3. Where do you need to be rescued by God?

4. Where does God want to grow and challenge you this week?

5. What is one word that you would use to describe God this week?

Focus Verse

May these words of my mouth and this meditation of my heart be pleasing in Your sight, Lord, my Rock and my Redeemer.
Psalm 19:14

Create

How has God rescued you?

- Write a poem or song describing how God has rescued you.
- Cut out words from old magazines of rescue, help, and relief and Modpodge them onto a box.
- Draw or paint an expression of God as a rescuer.
- Build something that brings freedom.

Care

Rescue something

- Have coffee or tea with someone and ask where God has rescued them.
- Go to an animal shelter and rescue an animal.
- Rescue all the lost socks in your house and find their matches!

Focus Verse

1. Find a quiet place to sit with your Bible and journal.

2.Close your eyes, take a deep breath, invite Jesus to center you in His truth and hold you in His love with this exercise:

- ○ Put your hands together, fingers pointing away from you, and say:
  Center me in Your truth.
- ○ Fold your hands together, squeeze, and say:
  Hold me in Your love.
- ○ Take another deep breath, open your eyes.

Read your focus verse for the week.

Say your focus verse for the week.

Write your focus verse for the week.

Daily Strategy

Read Psalms Chapter 16

Work with this verse: Psalm 16:5

1. **Print:** Write out the verse(s)
2. **Pronounce**: Read the verse(s) out loud
3. **Pause**: Reread the verse(s) and pause on each word or phrase
4. **Pinpoint:** Circle or underline the words that jump out at you
5. **Personalize:** Place your life events into each phrase
6. **Pour:** Write each section you personalized into a prayer

Use this space below or your own prayer journal.

Focus Verse

1. Find a quiet place to sit with your Bible and journal.

2. Close your eyes, take a deep breath, invite Jesus to center you in His truth and hold you in His love with this exercise:

- ○ Put your hands together, fingers pointing away from you, and say:
  Center me in Your truth.
- ○ Fold your hands together, squeeze, and say:
  Hold me in Your love.
- ○ Take another deep breath, open your eyes.

Read your focus verse for the week.

Say your focus verse for the week.

Write your focus verse for the week.

Daily Strategy

Read Psalms Chapter 17

Work with this verse: Psalm 17:2

1. **Print:** Write out the verse(s)
2. **Pronounce**: Read the verse(s) out loud
3. **Pause**: Reread the verse(s) and pause on each word or phrase
4. **Pinpoint:** Circle or underline the words that jump out at you
5. **Personalize:** Place your life events into each phrase
6. **Pour:** Write each section you personalized into a prayer

Use this space below or your own prayer journal.

Focus Verse

1. Find a quiet place to sit with your Bible and journal.

2. Close your eyes, take a deep breath, invite Jesus to center you in His truth and hold you in His love with this exercise:

- Put your hands together, fingers pointing away from you, and say:
  Center me in Your truth.
- Fold your hands together, squeeze, and say:
  Hold me in Your love.
- Take another deep breath, open your eyes.

Read your focus verse for the week.

Say your focus verse for the week.

Write your focus verse for the week.

Daily Strategy

Read Psalms Chapter 18

Work with this verse: Psalm 18:5

1. **Print:** Write out the verse(s)
2. **Pronounce**: Read the verse(s) out loud
3. **Pause**: Reread the verse(s) and pause on each word or phrase
4. **Pinpoint:** Circle or underline the words that jump out at you
5. **Personalize:** Place your life events into each phrase
6. **Pour:** Write each section you personalized into a prayer

Use this space below or your own prayer journal.

PRINT
POUR
PRONOUNCE
PERSONALIZE
PAUSE
PINPOINT

Focus Verse

1. Find a quiet place to sit with your Bible and journal.

2. Close your eyes, take a deep breath, invite Jesus to center you in His truth and hold you in His love with this exercise:

- ○ Put your hands together, fingers pointing away from you, and say:
  Center me in Your truth.
- ○ Fold your hands together, squeeze, and say:
  Hold me in Your love.
- ○ Take another deep breath, open your eyes.

Read your focus verse for the week.
Say your focus verse for the week.
Write your focus verse for the week.

Daily Strategy

Read Psalms Chapter 19

Work with this verse: Psalm 19:14

1. **Print:** Write out the verse(s)
2. **Pronounce**: Read the verse(s) out loud
3. **Pause**: Reread the verse(s) and pause on each word or phrase
4. **Pinpoint:** Circle or underline the words that jump out at you
5. **Personalize:** Place your life events into each phrase
6. **Pour:** Write each section you personalized into a prayer

Use this space below or your own prayer journal.

Focus Verse

1. Find a quiet place to sit with your Bible and journal.

2. Close your eyes, take a deep breath, invite Jesus to center you in His truth and hold you in His love with this exercise:

- ○ Put your hands together, fingers pointing away from you, and say:
  Center me in Your truth.
- ○ Fold your hands together, squeeze, and say:
  Hold me in Your love.
- ○ Take another deep breath, open your eyes.

Read your focus verse for the week.

Say your focus verse for the week.

Write your focus verse for the week.

GOD KNOWS WHEN YOU ARE ANXIOUS

Daily Strategy

Read Psalms Chapter 20

Work with this verse: Psalm 20:4

1. **Print:** Write out the verse(s)
2. **Pronounce**: Read the verse(s) out loud
3. **Pause**: Reread the verse(s) and pause on each word or phrase
4. **Pinpoint:** Circle or underline the words that jump out at you
5. **Personalize:** Place your life events into each phrase
6. **Pour:** Write each section you personalized into a prayer

Use this space below or your own prayer journal.

Week 5

Strength

Psalms 21-25

"——

GOD, PLEASE GIVE ME PATIENCE,
IF YOU GIVE ME STRENGTH,
I WILL JUST PUNCH THEM IN THE NOSE.

Ha
Ha Ha
Ha
Ha Ha

Learn With Lisa
WK 5 Teaching Notes

Strength

**Everlasting God
(Strength Will Rise)**
By Chris Tomlin

Talk & Share

Discussion Questions:

1. Which Psalm was powerful in your life this week?

2. When was a time in your life when you felt strong?

3. Where do you need God's strength right now?

4. How is God's power different from anything else in this world?

5. How can the Psalms help you connect with God's strength this week?

Focus Verse

Show me your ways, Lord, teach me your paths. Guide me in Your truth and teach me, for You are God, my Savior, and my hope is in You all day long.
Psalm 25:4-5

Create

When has God been your strength?

- Write a poem or song describing how God has been your strength.
- How many songs can you find about strength?
- Draw or paint an expression of God's strength.
- Build something strong.

Care

Be strong for someone

- Take someone to lunch who needs to be reminded that God is strong when feeling weak.
- What can you do for someone vulnerable?
- Play a game of Jenga with someone and reflect on which pieces are strong and which are weak.

Focus Verse

1. Find a quiet place to sit with your Bible and journal.

2. Close your eyes, take a deep breath, invite Jesus to center you in His truth and hold you in His love with this exercise:

- ○ Put your hands together, fingers pointing away from you, and say:
  Center me in Your truth.
- ○ Fold your hands together, squeeze, and say:
  Hold me in Your love.
- ○ Take another deep breath, open your eyes.

Read your focus verse for the week.

Say your focus verse for the week.

Write your focus verse for the week.

GOD KNOWS WHEN YOU ARE ANXIOUS

Daily Strategy

Read Psalms Chapter 21

Work with this verse: Psalm 21:13

1. **Print:** Write out the verse(s)
2. **Pronounce**: Read the verse(s) out loud
3. **Pause**: Reread the verse(s) and pause on each word or phrase
4. **Pinpoint:** Circle or underline the words that jump out at you
5. **Personalize:** Place your life events into each phrase
6. **Pour:** Write each section you personalized into a prayer

Use this space below or your own prayer journal.

Focus Verse

1. Find a quiet place to sit with your Bible and journal.

2. Close your eyes, take a deep breath, invite Jesus to center you in His truth and hold you in His love with this exercise:

- ○ Put your hands together, fingers pointing away from you, and say:
  Center me in Your truth.
- ○ Fold your hands together, squeeze, and say:
  Hold me in Your love.
- ○ Take another deep breath, open your eyes.

Read your focus verse for the week.

Say your focus verse for the week.

Write your focus verse for the week.

Daily Strategy

Read Psalms Chapter 22

Work with this verse: Psalm 22:19

1. **Print:** Write out the verse(s)
2. **Pronounce**: Read the verse(s) out loud
3. **Pause**: Reread the verse(s) and pause on each word or phrase
4. **Pinpoint:** Circle or underline the words that jump out at you
5. **Personalize:** Place your life events into each phrase
6. **Pour:** Write each section you personalized into a prayer

Use this space below or your own prayer journal.

Focus Verse

1. Find a quiet place to sit with your Bible and journal.

2. Close your eyes, take a deep breath, invite Jesus to center you in His truth and hold you in His love with this exercise:

- Put your hands together, fingers pointing away from you, and say:
  Center me in Your truth.
- Fold your hands together, squeeze, and say:
  Hold me in Your love.
- Take another deep breath, open your eyes.

Read your focus verse for the week.

Say your focus verse for the week.

Write your focus verse for the week.

Daily Strategy

Read Psalms Chapter 23

Work with this verse: Psalm 23:1-3

1. **Print:** Write out the verse(s)
2. **Pronounce**: Read the verse(s) out loud
3. **Pause**: Reread the verse(s) and pause on each word or phrase
4. **Pinpoint:** Circle or underline the words that jump out at you
5. **Personalize:** Place your life events into each phrase
6. **Pour:** Write each section you personalized into a prayer

Use this space below or your own prayer journal.

Focus Verse

1. Find a quiet place to sit with your Bible and journal.

2. Close your eyes, take a deep breath, invite Jesus to center you in His truth and hold you in His love with this exercise:

- Put your hands together, fingers pointing away from you, and say:
  Center me in Your truth.
- Fold your hands together, squeeze, and say:
  Hold me in Your love.
- Take another deep breath, open your eyes.

Read your focus verse for the week.

Say your focus verse for the week.

Write your focus verse for the week.

Daily Strategy

Read Psalms Chapter 24

Work with this verse: Psalm 24:1

1. **Print:** Write out the verse(s)
2. **Pronounce**: Read the verse(s) out loud
3. **Pause**: Reread the verse(s) and pause on each word or phrase
4. **Pinpoint:** Circle or underline the words that jump out at you
5. **Personalize:** Place your life events into each phrase
6. **Pour:** Write each section you personalized into a prayer

PRINT

POUR

PRONOUNCE

PERSONALIZE

PAUSE

PINPOINT

Use this space below or your own prayer journal.

Focus Verse

1. Find a quiet place to sit with your Bible and journal.

2. Close your eyes, take a deep breath, invite Jesus to center you in His truth and hold you in His love with this exercise:

- Put your hands together, fingers pointing away from you, and say:
  Center me in Your truth.
- Fold your hands together, squeeze, and say:
  Hold me in Your love.
- Take another deep breath, open your eyes.

Read your focus verse for the week.

Say your focus verse for the week.

Write your focus verse for the week.

GOD KNOWS WHEN YOU ARE ANXIOUS

Daily Strategy

Read Psalms Chapter 25

Work with this verse: Psalm 25:24-25

1. **Print:** Write out the verse(s)
2. **Pronounce**: Read the verse(s) out loud
3. **Pause**: Reread the verse(s) and pause on each word or phrase
4. **Pinpoint:** Circle or underline the words that jump out at you
5. **Personalize:** Place your life events into each phrase
6. **Pour:** Write each section you personalized into a prayer

Use this space below or your own prayer journal.

Week 6

Trust

Psalms 26-30

> *NEVER TRUST STAIRS*
> *THEY ARE ALWAYS UP TO SOMETHING.*

Ha Ha Ha Ha Ha

Learn With Lisa
WK 6 Teaching Notes

I Will Trust In You
By Lauren Daigle

Talk & Share

Discussion Questions:

1. Which Psalm did you most connect with this week?

2. Is there a particular area in which you are struggling to trust the Lord in your own life?

3. Who is someone you trust and why?

4. How does trust impact our relationships?

5. How does trust give you confidence and fight your anxiety?

Focus Verse

Wait for the Lord;
be strong and take heart
and wait for the Lord.
Psalm 27:14

Create

What do you trust God with?

- Write a poem or song describing how you will trust God.
- Write out the word TRUST and make a word collage of all the thing and people you want to trust God with.
- Draw or paint an expression of how you will trust God.
- Build something that holds something like God holds your trust.

Care

Be trustworthy for someone

- Listen to someone share their heart. Keep it just between the two of you.
- Let 1-2 people know you trust them and thank them for being there.
- Who do you want to build more trust with? Be consistent in showing up for them in some way.

Focus Verse

1. Find a quiet place to sit with your Bible and journal.

2. Close your eyes, take a deep breath, invite Jesus to center you in His truth and hold you in His love with this exercise:

- Put your hands together, fingers pointing away from you, and say:
  Center me in Your truth.
- Fold your hands together, squeeze, and say:
  Hold me in Your love.
- Take another deep breath and open your eyes.

Read your focus verse for the week.
Say your focus verse for the week.
Write your focus verse for the week.

GOD KNOWS WHEN YOU ARE ANXIOUS

Daily Strategy

Read Psalms Chapter 26

Work with this verse: Psalm 26:2-3

1. **Print:** Write out the verse(s)
2. **Pronounce**: Read the verse(s) out loud
3. **Pause**: Reread the verse(s) and pause on each word or phrase
4. **Pinpoint:** Circle or underline the words that jump out at you
5. **Personalize:** Place your life events into each phrase
6. **Pour:** Write each section you personalized into a prayer

Use this space below or your own prayer journal.

Focus Verse

1. Find a quiet place to sit with your Bible and journal.

2. Close your eyes, take a deep breath, invite Jesus to center you in His truth and hold you in His love with this exercise:

- ○ Put your hands together, fingers pointing away from you, and say:
  Center me in Your truth.
- ○ Fold your hands together, squeeze, and say:
  Hold me in Your love.
- ○ Take another deep breath and open your eyes.

Read your focus verse for the week.
Say your focus verse for the week.
Write your focus verse for the week.

Daily Strategy

Read Psalms Chapter 27

Work with this verse: Psalm 27:14

1. **Print:** Write out the verse(s)
2. **Pronounce**: Read the verse(s) out loud
3. **Pause**: Reread the verse(s) and pause on each word or phrase
4. **Pinpoint:** Circle or underline the words that jump out at you
5. **Personalize:** Place your life events into each phrase
6. **Pour:** Write each section you personalized into a prayer

Use this space below or your own prayer journal.

Focus Verse

1. Find a quiet place to sit with your Bible and journal.

2. Close your eyes, take a deep breath, invite Jesus to center you in His truth and hold you in His love with this exercise:

- o Put your hands together, fingers pointing away from you, and say:
  Center me in Your truth.
- o Fold your hands together, squeeze, and say:
  Hold me in Your love.
- o Take another deep breath, open your eyes.

Read your focus verse for the week.
Say your focus verse for the week.
Write your focus verse for the week.

Daily Strategy

Read Psalms Chapter 28

Work with this verse: Psalm 28:7

1. **Print:** Write out the verse(s)
2. **Pronounce**: Read the verse(s) out loud
3. **Pause**: Reread the verse(s) and pause on each word or phrase
4. **Pinpoint:** Circle or underline the words that jump out at you
5. **Personalize:** Place your life events into each phrase
6. **Pour:** Write each section you personalized into a prayer

POUR
PRINT
PRONOUNCE
PERSONALIZE
PAUSE
PINPOINT

Use this space below or your own prayer journal.

Focus Verse

1. Find a quiet place to sit with your Bible and journal.

2. Close your eyes, take a deep breath, invite Jesus to center you in His truth and hold you in His love with this exercise:

   - Put your hands together, fingers pointing away from you, and say:
     Center me in Your truth.
   - Fold your hands together, squeeze, and say:
     Hold me in Your love.
   - Take another deep breath and open your eyes.

Read your focus verse for the week.
Say your focus verse for the week.
Write your focus verse for the week.

Daily Strategy

Read Psalms Chapter 29

Work with this verse: Psalm 29:11

1. **Print:** Write out the verse(s)
2. **Pronounce**: Read the verse(s) out loud
3. **Pause**: Reread the verse(s) and pause on each word or phrase
4. **Pinpoint:** Circle or underline the words that jump out at you
5. **Personalize:** Place your life events into each phrase
6. **Pour:** Write each section you personalized into a prayer

Use this space below or your own prayer journal.

Focus Verse

1. Find a quiet place to sit with your Bible and journal.

2. Close your eyes, take a deep breath, invite Jesus to center you in His truth and hold you in His love with this exercise:

- ○ Put your hands together, fingers pointing away from you, and say:
  Center me in Your truth.
- ○ Fold your hands together, squeeze, and say:
  Hold me in Your love.
- ○ Take another deep breath and open your eyes.

Read your focus verse for the week.
Say your focus verse for the week.
Write your focus verse for the week.

Daily Strategy

Read Psalms Chapter 30

Work with this verse: Psalm 30:2

1. **Print:** Write out the verse(s)
2. **Pronounce**: Read the verse(s) out loud
3. **Pause**: Reread the verse(s) and pause on each word or phrase
4. **Pinpoint:** Circle or underline the words that jump out at you
5. **Personalize:** Place your life events into each phrase
6. **Pour:** Write each section you personalized into a prayer

PRINT

POUR

PRONOUNCE

PERSONALIZE

PAUSE

PINPOINT

Use this space below or your own prayer journal.

Week 7

Blessings

*I'M READY FOR SOME BLESSINGS
THAT AREN'T IN DISGUISE!*

Ha Ha Ha Ha Ha Ha

Learn With Lisa
WK 7 Teaching Notes

WK 7 Blessings

10,00 Reasons (Bless The Lord)
By Matt Redman

Talk & Share

Discussion Questions:

1. How has this study of the Psalms blessed your life?

2. What has been one of the most impactful things you have gained through this study?

3. How has reading the Psalms helped you understand God differently?

4. How has using the NIV and The Message been helpful in this study to you?

5. How can you use the Psalms to help you with your anxiety?

Congratulations
You did it! **Oh Yeah?**
YES! ►AMAZING◄ **YAY!**

How did the Lord work through this study in your life?

I want to hear about it!

● **REC** Please send me an email or video message to **lisatoney@gmail.com**.

I love so much to hear how God is working. I read/listen to every single one.

Get others excited about this study!

★★★★★

Review this product
Share your thoughts with other customers

Write a customer review

- Leave a review on Amazon! Type this book title into Amazon, then scroll down to "Customer Review" and share the love!

- Post a photo of yourself on your social media with this book cover and share how being **KNOWN** by God impacts your life.

I'm so proud of you!
You are invited to join us for our next study **SEEN** of Psalms 31–60.

LisaToney.com/seen

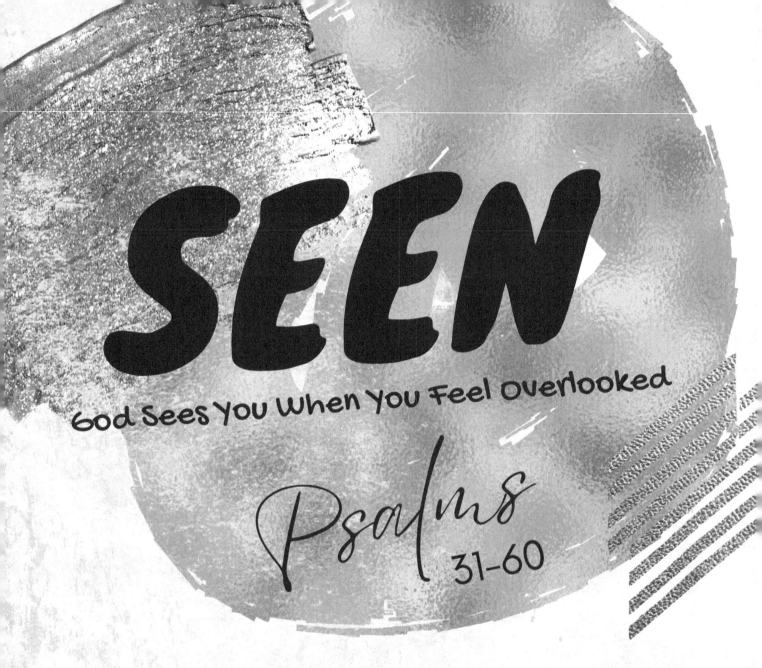

SEEN

God Sees You When You Feel Overlooked

Psalms
31-60

A Faith Habits Bible Study
Lisa Toney

lisatoney.com/seen

Made in the USA
Coppell, TX
09 December 2024

42110204R00063